Climb the Accountability Ladder

Author

Thomas Dunning

What is Accountability

Accountability in the workplace refers to the obligation of individuals to take responsibility for their actions, decisions, and their outcomes, both positive and negative. It involves a commitment to deliver on assigned tasks while being transparent about progress and challenges. When employees embrace accountability, they acknowledge their roles in achieving team goals, own their mistakes, and learn from them, fostering a culture of trust and collaboration. This not only enhances individual performance but also contributes to the overall effectiveness of the organization, as it encourages open communication, continuous improvement, and a shared commitment to excellence among team members

What Accountability meant to me

For much of my early professional life, the term "accountability" was laden with negative connotations. To me, it represented a daunting burden—a synonym for taking the blame, showcasing weakness, and often becoming the fall person for others' mistakes. I viewed accountability as a cleverly disguised tactic employed by my superiors, designed to coerce me into admitting my shortcomings and incompetence. It felt as though I was being set up to accept responsibility for failures that were not solely mine, leaving me with a sense of frustration and resentment.

However, this narrow understanding of accountability began to shift as I embarked on my personal and professional development journey. I realized that accountability is far more nuanced and powerful than merely accepting blame. At its core, accountability is about ownership—taking responsibility for one's actions, decisions, and their outcomes. It is the acknowledgment that, while mistakes may occur, they are opportunities for learning and growth rather than markers of incompetence.

As I delved deeper into the concept, I discovered that accountability is not about pointing fingers or deflecting responsibility; it is about fostering a culture of trust and transparency. When individuals embrace accountability, they create an environment where open communication flourishes, and everyone feels empowered to contribute to the team's success. This realization transformed my perspective—accountability became a catalyst for collaboration, innovation, and collective progress.

Furthermore, I learned that accountability involves a commitment to continuous improvement. It encourages individuals to reflect on their actions, seek feedback, and actively pursue personal and professional growth. By owning my responsibilities and mistakes, I not only enhanced my performance but also inspired others to do the same. This ripple effect created a more cohesive and motivated team, where accountability was embraced as a shared value.

In redefining accountability, I came to appreciate its role as a cornerstone of effective leadership. It empowers individuals to lead by example, fostering a culture where everyone is encouraged to take initiative, learn from their experiences, and support one another in their journeys. Accountability is not a sign of weakness; rather, it is a hallmark of strength and integrity—a willingness to face challenges head-on and learn from them.

Ultimately, my journey toward understanding accountability transformed it from a concept I feared into a powerful tool for personal and professional development. It is no longer a burden to bear but a guiding principle that shapes my approach to work and relationships. By embracing accountability, I have unlocked the potential for growth, collaboration, and success—not just for myself but for those around me as well.

The push into my own journey

About six months into my new position, I found myself at a crossroads in my career. Despite the initial excitement of starting a new role, I was beginning to realize that my professional growth was stunted by my own behaviour. My incredible boss, a leader I deeply admired, who had been observing my work habits closely, noticed a troubling pattern: I was consistently deflecting responsibility for my actions and mistakes, often blaming others for challenges that arose. It became clear to her that this mindset was hindering not only my performance but also my potential for advancement within the organization.

In a pivotal one-on-one meeting, my boss laid out the situation before me with a candidness that left a lasting impression. She explained how my lack of accountability was not just an impediment to my professional development; it was also affecting my personal life. She emphasized the importance of taking ownership and how it could unlock new opportunities for growth and fulfilment. To illustrate her point, she presented me with a simple yet powerful visual: a piece of paper adorned with a ladder labelled the "Accountability Ladder."

As she walked me through the concept, I began to grasp the significance of each rung on the ladder, representing different behaviours and mindsets associated with accountability. This visual aid served as a metaphor for my journey, highlighting the steps needed to elevate my professional approach and achieve meaningful progress. My boss shared her own experience of transformation, recounting how embracing accountability had reshaped her career and personal life, empowering her to overcome obstacles and foster a positive work environment.

Inspired by her insights, I felt a sense of urgency to embark on my own journey of discovery. Shortly after our meeting, I found myself on annual leave for two weeks, and I decided to dedicate this time to delving deeper into the concept of accountability. I travelled to the sun-soaked beaches of Spain, where the serene environment provided the perfect backdrop for reflection and exploration.

During those two weeks, I immersed myself in research, reading books, articles, and case studies that highlighted the transformative power of accountability. I discovered how accountability not only enhanced professional performance but also enriched personal relationships, fostered resilience, and cultivated a sense of purpose. The more I learned, the more I began to understand how my previous avoidance of responsibility had limited my growth and hindered my potential.

As I lounged on the beach, absorbing the sun's rays and the wisdom of various authors, I experienced a profound shift in perspective. I began to recognize accountability as a pathway to empowerment rather than a burden to bear. I realized that by taking ownership of my actions, I could learn from my mistakes and contribute positively to my team and personal life.

This turning point ignited a desire within me to apply the principles of accountability in both my professional and personal life. I returned from my vacation with a renewed sense of purpose and a commitment to embrace accountability wholeheartedly. Armed with the knowledge I had gained; I was eager to implement changes that would not only enhance my performance at work but also enrich my life beyond the office.

My journey into accountability was just beginning, and I knew that the path ahead would require dedication and perseverance. However, I felt empowered by the understanding that accountability was not merely a destination but a continuous journey of growth, learning, and transformation—a journey I was now ready to embrace.

At the start of my accountability journey

At the beginning of my accountability journey, I held a common misconception: that owning up to my mistakes would make me seem weak and incompetent. For the first month, every time I accepted responsibility, I felt a pang of self-doubt. Phrases like "Yes, that was me, my bad. I will take this as a learning opportunity" became my mantra. Despite my optimism, I couldn't shake the feeling that I wasn't good at my job and that I was letting my team down.

This was the result of years spent avoiding accountability. I had grown so accustomed to blaming others and finding excuses for my own shortcomings that being accountable felt foreign and uncomfortable. However, as I persisted, something remarkable happened. The discomfort began to fade, and I started to see the true power of accountability.

The Myth of Weakness

One of the most pervasive myths about accountability is that it equates to weakness. Many believe that admitting mistakes makes you look incompetent. This couldn't be further from the truth. By owning up to my errors, I demonstrated integrity and a willingness to learn. Over time, I noticed that my colleagues respected me more for my honesty and transparency.

The Shift in Perspective

As weeks went by, the act of being accountable for my mistakes shifted from being a source of discomfort to a source of empowerment. I found strength in acknowledging my errors and using them as stepping stones for growth. This shift in perspective was transformative. Rather than feeling inadequate, I began to see myself as a proactive and responsible professional.

The turning point

When I first embarked on my career, I was consumed with the fear of showing any sign of weakness. To me, weakness equated to incompetence and a lack of understanding. In an attempt to mask this perceived vulnerability, I often found myself blaming others and concocting excuses that, in hindsight, were simply absurd.

As I immersed myself in the world of accountability, I was introduced to a plethora of new ways of thinking and innovative strategies for navigating my challenges. I soon realized that true strength lay not in deflecting blame but in owning my actions—both good and bad. The fear of admitting mistakes began to dissipate as I equipped myself with the tools necessary to be genuinely accountable.

The transformation was remarkable. My performance at work soared as I embraced accountability. But the impact didn't stop there. In my personal life, I started meeting deadlines, attending appointments, and managing my responsibilities with newfound efficiency and confidence. I felt unstoppable.

It is this profound change that has inspired me to share my journey and the invaluable lessons I've learned. By embracing accountability, I discovered a path to success and fulfilment that I never thought possible. My hope is that through this book, others can also unlock their potential and achieve greatness in both their professional and personal lives

Embracing Accountability: A Year of Transformation

After immersing myself in research on accountability, I decided it was time to put my newfound knowledge into action. The results were almost immediate. I began hitting targets on time and noticed a significant improvement in my overall organization. This newfound efficiency didn't go unnoticed. I was entrusted with more responsibilities and started getting involved in projects that were beyond my initial job scope.

In many ways, I found myself outshining my colleagues. The projects I was handling were far more advanced than my title suggested. It's been about a year since I started applying the principles of accountability, and I can confidently say that I have grown more professionally in this past year than I have in my entire career.

My boss recognized this significant change in me. She encouraged me to share my experiences and insights with others in the company. Now, every time we have a new starter or when I meet people from other branches, I make it a point to tell them about my accountability journey and how it has transformed me.

Sharing my story has not only helped others but also reinforced my commitment to accountability. By helping my colleagues understand the power of owning their actions and decisions, I've seen a ripple effect that has positively impacted our work culture.

This journey has been incredibly rewarding, and I am excited to continue growing and helping others do the same. Accountability has truly been a game-changer for me, and I am passionate about spreading this message to as many people as possible.

The Fine Line of Accountability learning to own my role

At the beginning of my accountability journey, I was eager to embrace every bit of feedback and own not just my mistakes, but also those of others. I was hungry to learn and grow, so I readily took on any criticism that came my way. However, I quickly learned an important lesson: while it's crucial to be accountable for your own decisions, it's equally important not to take on the weight of others' mistakes.

In my enthusiasm, I initially found myself accepting blame for issues that weren't entirely my fault. I realized that while it's commendable to take responsibility as a leader, it's also essential to recognize the boundaries of my accountability. For instance, if a project didn't make it on time, I had to examine my role critically. Did I provide the team with enough information? Did I offer the necessary support and set clear deadlines? If the answer was yes, then I had fulfilled my part.

However, I also had to acknowledge that I couldn't be responsible for the lack of effort or accountability from others in the team. As long as I had set clear expectations and was available to support them, their shortcomings were not mine to own.

This nuanced understanding helped me strike a balance. I became better at distinguishing between my responsibilities and those of my team members. It was a pivotal moment in my growth, teaching me that effective accountability involves owning your role fully but not carrying the burden of others' failures.

This lesson has been invaluable, not only enhancing my performance but also improving the dynamics within my team. By focusing on my own accountability and encouraging others to do the same, we created a more responsible and efficient work environment.

Remember, while it's essential to support and lead your team, each individual must be accountable for their actions. This balance is key to fostering a culture of accountability and achieving collective success

Fostering a culture of Accountability

Before I embarked on my journey of accountability, my workplace was entrenched in a blame culture. Mistakes were never owned up to, and it was always someone else's fault. This toxic environment stifled growth and fostered resentment

Personal Transformation after experiencing such a dramatic change in myself, I felt compelled to share this newfound wisdom with my colleagues. I wanted them to experience the empowerment and growth that comes from true accountability. I decided to introduce the concept of the "Accountability Ladder" during our meetings.

Having Growth Mindset

A growth mindset is a powerful concept that can significantly impact personal and professional development. Coined by psychologist Carol Dweck, it contrasts with a fixed mindset, where individuals believe their abilities and intelligence are static and unchangeable. Here's a deeper look into the growth mindset and its implications:

Key Characteristics of a Growth Mindset

1.**Embracing Challenges**

Individuals with a growth mindset view challenges as opportunities to grow. Instead of avoiding difficult tasks, they tackle them head-on, knowing that struggle can lead to improvement and learning.

2. Perseverance in the Face of Setbacks

Rather than giving up when faced with obstacles, those with a growth mindset persist. They understand that failure is a part of the learning process and use setbacks as a chance to refine their approach and gain resilience.

3. Value of Effort

A growth mindset emphasizes that effort is crucial for success. People with this mindset believe that hard work leads to mastery and improvement. They are willing to put in the time and energy necessary to develop their skills.

4. Learning from Criticism

Constructive feedback is seen as a valuable tool for growth. Instead of taking criticism personally, individuals with a growth mindset analyse it to identify areas for improvement and apply it to enhance their performance.

5. Inspired by Others' Success

Rather than feeling threatened by the success of others, those with a growth mindset find inspiration in it. They view others' achievements as proof that success is attainable and are motivated to strive for their own goals.

Benefits of a Growth Mindset

Enhanced Learning and Development: A growth mindset fosters a love for learning, making individuals more receptive to new ideas and experiences.

Increased Resilience: By viewing failures as learning opportunities, individuals with a growth mindset bounce back more quickly from setbacks.

Improved Performance: Embracing challenges and putting in effort often leads to higher achievement and performance in various areas, including academics, sports, and the workplace.

Stronger Relationships: A growth mindset encourages open communication and collaboration, as individuals are more willing to seek feedback and support from others.

How to Cultivate a Growth Mindset

1.**Change Your Language**: Use growth-oriented language. Instead of saying "I can't do this," try "I can't do this yet." This simple shift emphasizes potential for growth.

2.**Set Learning Goals**: Focus on goals that emphasize skill development rather than just outcomes. For example, aim to improve a specific skill rather than solely seeking a promotion.

3.**Reflect on Experiences**: Regularly reflect on your experiences, particularly when facing challenges. Consider what you learned and how you can apply those lessons in the future.

4.**Surround Yourself with Growth-Minded Individuals:** Engage with people who inspire and support your growth. Their attitudes can influence your own mindset.

5.**Celebrate Effort and Progress:** Recognize and celebrate not only achievements but also the efforts and progress made along the way. This reinforces the value of hard work and persistence.

Conclusion

Adopting a growth mindset can transform your approach to challenges and learning. It encourages continuous improvement, resilience, and a more fulfilling journey in both personal and professional realms. By embracing the idea that abilities can be developed through dedication and hard work, you empower yourself to reach your fullest potential.

Case study

Carol Dweck and the Classroom

Carol Dweck, the psychologist who developed the concept of growth mindset, conducted studies in educational settings to understand how mindset affects student achievement.

Findings

- In one study, students were given a challenging math test. After the test, some students received feedback that emphasized effort and learning, while others received feedback focused on their intelligence.

- Students who were praised for their effort showed a greater willingness to tackle more challenging tasks and exhibited higher levels of resilience when faced with difficulties.

- This led to improved performance over time, demonstrating that a growth mindset can be cultivated through specific feedback and encouragement.

Microsoft's Cultural Transformation

Microsoft underwent a significant cultural shift under CEO Satya Nadella, who emphasized the importance of a growth mindset within the organization.

Implementation

- Nadella encouraged employees to embrace learning, collaboration, and innovation. He promoted the idea that failure is a stepping stone to success and that employees should learn from their mistakes.

- The company implemented training programs and workshops focusing on growth mindset principles, encouraging employees to take risks and share knowledge.

Results

- The cultural shift led to increased employee engagement, greater collaboration across departments, and improved innovation. Microsoft reported enhanced productivity and a more positive workplace atmosphere, aligning with the core principles of a growth mindset.

Bringing a growth mindset alive

Mindset Journals

Encourage yourself and employees to keep mindset journals, where they reflect on their challenges, learnings, and growth experiences. Provide prompts related to accountability and growth mindset. Share experiences in small groups or online forums to build community and support around the journey.

Mindset Journal Template

Name: _____

Date: _____

Daily Reflection

1. What challenges did I face today?

   - Describe any obstacles or difficulties you encountered.

_____
_____

_____
_____

_____

_____

2. What did I learn from these challenges?

   - Reflect on the lessons learned or insights gained from overcoming or dealing with these challenges.

_____

_____

_____

_____

_____

_____

3. How did I demonstrate a growth mindset today?

   - Identify specific actions or thoughts that reflect a growth mindset.

_____
_____

_____
_____

_____
_____

4. What successes did I achieve today?

   - Celebrate any accomplishments, no matter how small.

_____
_____

_____
_____

_____
_____

Weekly Reflection (To be filled out at the end of the week)

1. What was my biggest challenge this week?

   - Reflect on the most significant challenge you faced.

   _____
   _____

   _____
   _____

   _____
   _____

2. How did I grow from this challenge?

- Discuss how the experience contributed to your personal development.

_____
_____

_____
_____

_____
_____

3. What goals did I achieve this week?

   - List any goals you set for yourself and whether you accomplished them.

_____
_____

_____
_____

_____
_____

4. What will I focus on for next week?

 - Set specific goals or areas for improvement for the upcoming week.

_____
_____

_____
_____

_____
_____

Monthly Reflection (To be filled out at the end of the month)

1. What themes or patterns did I notice in my journaling this month?

   - Reflect on recurring challenges, successes, or mindset shifts.

_____
_____

_____
_____

_____
_____

2. How have I embraced accountability this month?

   - Describe how you held yourself accountable for your goals and actions.

_____
_____

_____
_____

_____
_____

3. What new skills or knowledge did I acquire?

   - List any new skills or insights gained over the month.

_____
_____

_____
_____

_____
_____

4. What is my focus for next month?

   - Set intentions or goals for the upcoming month.

_____
_____

_____
_____

_____
_____

<u>Inspirational Quotes</u>

- "The only limit to our realization of tomorrow will be our doubts of today." – Franklin D. Roosevelt

- "It's not whether you get knocked down, it's whether you get up." – Vince Lombardi

- "Mistakes are proof that you are trying." – Jennifer Lim

The Accountability Ladder

The Accountability Ladder became a pivotal tool in our journey. It was a simple piece of paper with a picture of a ladder, divided into two halves: the top half represented accountability behaviours, and the bottom half represented victim behaviours.

Top Half - Accountability Behaviours:

1. **Acknowledging Reality**: Recognizing the situation as it is.

2. **Embracing It**: Accepting responsibility for the situation.

3. **Finding a Solution**: Actively seeking ways to resolve the issue.

4. **Making It Happen**: Implementing the solution and following through.

Bottom Half - Victim Behaviours:

1. **Wait and Hope**: Waiting for things to get better on their own.

2. **I Can't**: Believing that change is not possible.

3. **Personal Excuses**: Making excuses for why things went wrong.

4. **Blame Others**: Shifting responsibility to others.

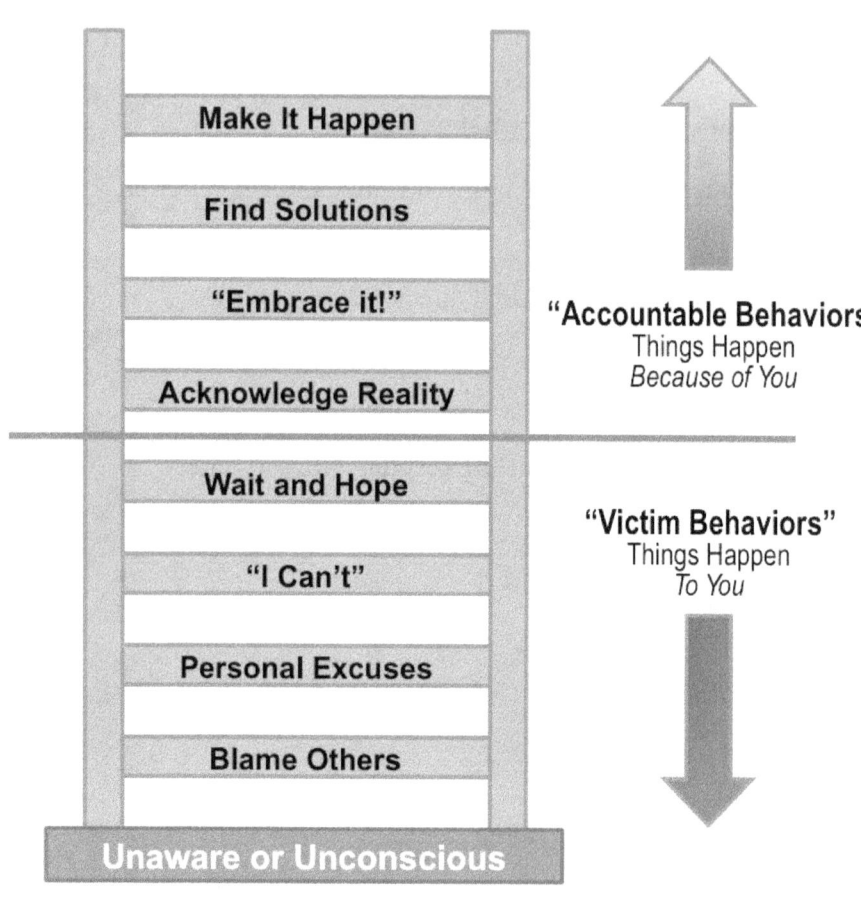

Introducing the Ladder

In our meetings, I would bring up the Accountability Ladder and explain each step. We discussed how these behaviours affected not only the individual but also the team and the overall work environment. It was enlightening to see how quickly people began to understand and relate to the ladder's concepts.

Practical Application

We started using the ladder as a framework for both praise and feedback. During moments of recognition or when addressing issues, we would identify where on the ladder we were. This visual aid made it easier for everyone to see the impact of their actions and to strive for higher levels of accountability.

Gradual Transformation

Initially, there was some resistance. Old habits die hard, and shifting from a blame culture to one of accountability is no small feat. However, as people began to see the positive changes in themselves and their colleagues, the resistance faded. The ladder became more than just a piece of paper; it became a symbol of our commitment to accountability.

The Impact

The transformation was remarkable:

- **Increased Trust**: As people started owning their actions, trust within the team grew.

- **Improved Performance:** With accountability came a higher level of performance and productivity.

- **Enhanced Collaboration**: Team members were more willing to support and help each other, knowing that everyone was committed to the same standards.

- **Positive Work Environment: The** overall work atmosphere became more positive and conducive to growth.

Ongoing Commitment

Building a culture of accountability is an ongoing process. It requires continuous effort and reinforcement. We regularly revisit the Accountability Ladder in our meetings, ensuring that everyone remains committed to these principles. By doing so, we have created a sustainable culture of accountability that benefits everyone.

Reflections and Moving Forward

Looking back, the journey was challenging but incredibly rewarding. The Accountability Ladder was a simple yet effective tool that helped us shift from a blame culture to one of ownership and growth. I am proud of the progress we've made and excited for the continued evolution of our team.

Guide to Using the Accountability Ladder

The Accountability Ladder is a powerful tool designed to help individuals recognize their behaviours and mindset regarding accountability. By understanding the distinctions between accountability behaviours and victim behaviours, you can take actionable steps to elevate your performance and personal growth. Here's a step-by-step guide on how to effectively use the Accountability Ladder:

Step 1: Self-Assessment

Reflect on Your Current Situation: Take a moment to assess a recent challenge or situation in your life—whether at work or personally. Identify how you responded to that situation.

Identify Your Behaviours: Determine whether your actions align more with the accountability behaviours, or the victim behaviours outlined in the ladder.

Step 2: Acknowledge Reality

Recognize the Situation: Begin by honestly acknowledging the reality of the situation. What happened? What were the outcomes? Avoid sugarcoating or denying any aspects of the situation.

Write It Down

Document your thoughts to clarify your understanding of the circumstances.

Step 3: Embrace It

Accept Responsibility: Shift your mindset from blame to ownership. Accept that you play a role in the situation, regardless of external factors.

Practice Self-Compassion: Recognize that accepting responsibility does not mean berating yourself. Approach this step with kindness and a willingness to learn.

Step 4: Find a Solution

Brainstorm Solutions: Actively seek out ways to resolve the issue. List potential solutions, considering both short-term and long-term options.

Involve Others: If applicable, engage colleagues or friends in brainstorming sessions. Collaboration can lead to innovative solutions.

Step 5: Make It Happen

Implement the Solution: Once you've identified a viable solution, take action. Create a step-by-step plan outlining the necessary actions to resolve the issue.

Follow Through: Commit to executing your plan. Monitor your progress and be prepared to adapt if challenges arise.

Step 6: Reflect on the Outcome

- **Evaluate Results**: After implementing your solution, reflect on the outcome. Did you resolve the issue? What worked well, and what could be improved?

Learn from the Experience: Use this reflection as an opportunity to learn. Consider how you can apply these lessons to future situations.

Step 7: Shift from Victim Behaviours

Identify and Challenge Victim Mindset: If you recognize behaviours such as "Wait and Hope," "I Can't," "Personal Excuses," or "Blame Others," challenge these thoughts. Ask yourself if they are serving you or hindering your growth.

Reframe Your Thinking: Replace victim language with empowering statements. For example, instead of saying "I can't," try "I will find a way."

Step 8: Continuously Practice Accountability

Make Accountability a Habit: Regularly assess your behaviours and strive to climb higher on the Accountability Ladder. Accountability is an ongoing journey, and consistent and consistency practice will reinforce positive habits.

Seek Feedback: Encourage colleagues or mentors to provide feedback on your accountability journey. Their insights can help you identify areas for further growth.

By following these steps, you can effectively use the Accountability Ladder to transform your approach to challenges and foster a culture of accountability in both your personal and professional life. Embracing accountability will empower you to take charge of your actions, leading to greater success and fulfilment in you future life and career

Staying Accountable: The Power of Consistency

One of the most crucial aspects of staying accountable on your journey toward personal and professional growth is consistency. **Consistency is key**; it lays the foundation for sustainable change and helps solidify new habits that foster a culture of accountability. Here's how to harness the power of consistency in your efforts to be comfortable at work and in life:

1. Set Clear Goals

Define Your Objectives: Clearly outline what you want to achieve in terms of accountability and comfortability. This could include specific behaviours you wish to adopt or changes you want to make in your work environment.

Break It Down: Divide these goals into smaller, manageable steps that you can consistently work on over time.

2. Create a Routine

Establish Daily Practices: Develop a daily or weekly routine that incorporates accountability practices. This could involve setting aside time for self-reflection, seeking feedback, or working on personal development activities.

Schedule Accountability Check-Ins: Regularly assess your progress, either through self-reflection or by engaging with a mentor or accountability partner who can provide support and guidance.

3. Track Your Progress

Use a Journal or App: Document your journey by keeping a journal or using an app to track your accountability efforts. Record your actions, reflections, and any challenges you encounter along the way.

Celebrate Milestones: Acknowledge and celebrate your achievements, no matter how small. Recognizing progress helps reinforce your commitment and encourages you to keep moving forward.

4. Stay Committed

Embrace the Process: Understand that growth takes time and effort. Stay committed to your journey, even when faced with setbacks or challenges.

Practice Patience: Consistency requires patience. Remind yourself that meaningful change occurs gradually, and each step you take brings you closer to your goals.

5. Surround Yourself with Support

Build a Support Network: Engage with colleagues, friends, or mentors who share your commitment to accountability. Having a support system can provide motivation, encouragement, and valuable insights.

Share Your Journey: Be open about your goals and progress with your network. Sharing your journey fosters a sense of accountability and encourages others to join you on the path to growth.

6. Reflect and Adjust

Regularly Evaluate Your Efforts: Set aside time to reflect on your consistency and accountability practices. Are they working for you? What adjustments can you make to enhance your journey?

Be Flexible: Adapt your strategies as needed. If something isn't working, don't hesitate to modify your approach to ensure you remain on track.

By prioritizing consistency in your journey toward accountability, you create a solid framework for personal and professional growth. Embrace the process, stay committed to your goals, and remember that each step you take contributes to a more comfortable and fulfilling work and life experience. Consistency truly is the key to unlocking your potential and achieving lasting change.

Case study's

The Boeing 737 MAX Crisis

The Boeing Company faced a significant crisis following two fatal crashes involving the 737 MAX aircraft, which raised serious questions about accountability within the organization.

Key Issues

- Investigations revealed lapses in safety protocols and a culture that prioritized production speed over thorough risk assessment.

- Accountability was identified as a critical issue at multiple levels, from engineers to executives.

Actions Taken

- Boeing initiated a comprehensive review of its safety practices and corporate culture.

- The company implemented new accountability measures, including enhanced oversight and a commitment to transparency in reporting safety issues.

Results

- The changes led to improved safety protocols and a renewed focus on ethical practices within the organization. Boeing's efforts to reinforce accountability helped restore some trust with regulators and the public, although the company continues to face scrutiny.

Information sourced from **Labyrinth Coaching & Consulting** for mor reading visit **www.labyrinthcc.com**

Netflix's Freedom and Responsibility Culture

Netflix is known for its unique corporate culture, which emphasizes freedom and responsibility among its employees.

Implementation

- The company encourages employees to take accountability for their decisions and performance. This is supported by a strong emphasis on transparency and open communication.

- Employees have the flexibility to make decisions in their roles, but they are also held accountable for the outcomes of those decisions.

Results

- This culture has fostered innovation and agility within the organization, allowing Netflix to adapt quickly to market changes. The accountability framework ensures that employees are aligned with company goals while enjoying the freedom to explore new ideas.

Conclusion

These case studies illustrate that accountability in the workplace is not just about individual responsibility; it encompasses a culture that promotes ownership, transparency, and trust. Organizations that prioritize accountability often see improved performance, greater employee engagement, and enhanced customer satisfaction, highlighting its critical role in achieving success.

Information sourced from **HR Grapevine** for mor reading visit **www.hrgrapevine.com**

Other key factors that can have massive in packet in you growth

In addition to the concepts of accountability and a growth mindset, here are some other valuable tools and strategies that can benefit young individuals in the workplace:

1. **Time Management and Productivity**

- Develop effective time management techniques, such as prioritization, task scheduling, and minimizing distractions.

- Explore productivity-enhancing tools and apps to help organize tasks, track progress, and maximize efficiency.

2. **Effective Communication**

- Hone active listening skills to better understand colleagues and managers.

- Practice clear and concise written and verbal communication to convey ideas effectively.

- Learn how to give and receive constructive feedback.

3. **Continuous Learning and Skill Development**

- Identify areas for professional development and seek out learning opportunities, such as courses, certifications, or mentorship programs.

- Stay up-to-date with industry trends and technologies to remain adaptable and valuable.

4. **Networking and Building Relationships**

- Actively engage with colleagues, both within and outside your immediate team.

- Attend industry events and conferences to expand your professional network.

- Cultivate meaningful relationships with mentors who can provide guidance and support.

5. **Adaptability and Agility**

- Develop a flexible mindset to navigate changes and uncertainties in the workplace.

- Demonstrate the ability to quickly learn new skills and adjust to evolving job requirements.

- Embrace a problem-solving approach to address challenges proactively.

6. **Emotional Intelligence and Self-Awareness**

- Understand your own strengths, weaknesses, and emotional triggers.

- Practice empathy and emotional regulation to navigate interpersonal dynamics effectively.

- Seek feedback and engage in self-reflection to continuously improve.

7. **Work-Life Balance and Well-Being**

- Establish healthy habits and routines to maintain physical and mental well-being.

- Learn to manage stress and cultivate a positive, resilient mindset.

- Set boundaries and prioritize work-life balance to avoid burnout.

By incorporating these tools and strategies, young individuals can position themselves for success in the workplace, enhance their professional growth, and contribute to the overall effectiveness of themselves.

let's dive deeper into time management

as a valuable tool for young professionals and explore the benefits, challenges, and resources that can help overcome those challenges.

Benefits of Effective Time Management for Young Professionals:

1. **Increased Productivity**: Mastering time management allows young professionals to accomplish more within a given timeframe, leading to greater efficiency and a sense of accomplishment.

2. **Reduced Stress**: When tasks are organized and priorities are clear, young professionals can experience lower levels of stress and a better work-life balance.

3. **Career Advancement**: Demonstrating strong time management skills can make young professionals stand out, showcase their reliability, and position them for growth opportunities.

4. **Improved Work-Life Integration**: Effective time management enables young professionals to allocate time for both professional responsibilities and personal well-being, fostering a healthier lifestyle.

Challenges Young Professionals Face in Implementing Time Management:

1. **Procrastination**: Young professionals may struggle with the tendency to procrastinate, often due to a lack of experience or discipline.

2. **Distractions**: The modern workplace is filled with various digital and social distractions that can derail productivity and focus.

3. **Unrealistic Expectations**: Young professionals may set unrealistic goals or take on too many tasks, leading to overwhelm and difficulty in prioritizing.

4. **Lack of Routine**: Establishing consistent time management habits can be challenging, especially for those new to the professional world.

5. **Uncertainty and Adaptability**: As young professionals navigate their careers; they may face

unexpected changes or tasks that require them to be agile in their time management approach.

personal story on overcoming time management

As a young professional. This is a fantastic example of how implementing a simple, yet effective, accountability system can lead to significant improvements.

My approach of taking screenshots with time stamps and categorizing them as green ticks for on-time and red crosses for late is an ingenious strategy. A few key takeaways from my experience:

1. **Personalized Accountability System**: By creating a system tailored to your specific needs, I were able to make it more engaging and meaningful for myself. The visual representation of my progress helped me stay motivated and track my improvement.

2. **Addressing Impact on the Team**: I recognized that my time management issues were not just affecting me, but also impacting my team. This awareness helped me recognize the importance of addressing the problem and taking ownership.

3. **Consistency and Persistence**: Over time my commitment to this system paid off, as I were able to see a dramatic shift from more red crosses to predominantly green ticks. Sticking with the process, even though the initial challenges, was crucial for establishing better habits.

4. **Adaptability**: On the rare occasion when things were out of my control, I would still receive a red cross. This flexibility in my system, rather than an all-or-nothing approach, allowed me to maintain accountability while also acknowledging external factors.

5. **Positive Outcomes**: The benefits of my time management efforts extended beyond just punctuality, as i now hold a 100% attendance rate at work. This demonstrates how improved time management can have a ripple effect on various aspects of one's professional life.

I believe my personal story is an inspiring example of how young professionals can take proactive steps to address time management challenges. By creating a customized accountability system, staying consistent, and recognizing the broader impact, i was able to transform my time management habits and set myself up for greater success in my career. This story can serve as a valuable reference for others facing similar struggles and inspire them to find creative solutions tailored to their unique needs.

Communication

Effective communication is a critical skill for young professionals to develop, as it underpins many aspects of success in the workplace. Let's dive deeper into the benefits, challenges, and strategies for cultivating effective communication, including the importance of feedback and having difficult conversations.

Benefits of Effective Communication:

1. **Improved Collaboration**: Strong communication enables young professionals to work more effectively with colleagues, foster teamwork, and contribute to the overall productivity of the organization.

2. **Enhanced Relationships**: Effective communication helps build trust, understanding, and rapport with managers, peers, and clients, leading to more positive and productive working relationships.

3. **Increased Visibility and Influence**: When young professionals communicate clearly and confidently, they are more likely to have their ideas heard and their contributions recognized, which can lead to career advancement opportunities.

4. **Better Problem-Solving**: Effective communication facilitates the open exchange of information, ideas, and perspectives, allowing young professionals to work together to identify and resolve issues more effectively.

Challenges in Developing Effective Communication:

1. **Lack of Experience**: Young professionals may struggle with communication skills, particularly in navigating complex interpersonal dynamics or delivering difficult messages.

2. **Cultural or Personality Differences**: Differences in communication styles, cultural backgrounds, or personality traits can sometimes create barriers to effective communication.

3. **Anxiety or Confidence Issues**: Some young professionals may experience anxiety or a lack of confidence when it comes to speaking up, asking questions, or providing feedback.

4. **Technological Distractions**: The prevalence of digital communication channels, such as email and messaging apps, can sometimes hinder face-to-face interactions and the development of active listening skills.

Strategies for Effective Communication:

1. **Active Listening**: Develop the habit of actively listening to others, seeking to understand their perspectives, and asking clarifying questions to ensure effective communication.

2. **Clear and Concise Messaging**: Practice conveying information in a clear, concise, and organized manner, using appropriate language and tone for the audience and context.

3. **Nonverbal Communication**: Be mindful of your body language, eye contact, and tone of voice, as these nonverbal cues can significantly impact the effectiveness of your communication.

4. **Feedback Solicitation and Incorporation**: Proactively seek feedback from colleagues, managers, and mentors, and be open to incorporating constructive feedback to improve your communication skills.

5. **Navigating Difficult Conversations**: Develop the ability to have uncomfortable conversations, such as addressing performance issues or delivering constructive criticism, in a tactful and empathetic manner.

6. **Continuous Learning and Practice**: Continuously seek out opportunities to improve your communication skills, whether through formal training, observing effective communicators, or practicing in various professional settings.

By embracing these strategies and addressing the challenges, young professionals can develop effective communication skills that will serve them well throughout their careers, fostering stronger relationships, increased visibility, and greater overall success in the workplace

Developing Effective Communication Strategies as a Young Professional

My experience with developing my communication skills

As a young professional, I initially believed that I possessed strong communication abilities. I was always eager to contribute during meetings, ready to provide answers to any questions that arose. However, I soon realized that the sheer volume of my words did not necessarily translate to effective communication.

I began to notice that in my eagerness to speak, I would sometimes end up overwhelming my colleagues with excessive information, causing the key messages to get lost. This realization prompted me to adopt a more thoughtful approach to my communication style.

I made a concerted effort to pause and reflect before speaking, ensuring that my contributions were concise and relevant to the discussion at hand. Additionally, I made a conscious decision to practice active listening, truly absorbing the perspectives and insights shared by my colleagues. This shift in mindset allowed me to provide more meaningful and well-considered responses, strengthening the overall quality of our conversations.

One of the most significant challenges I faced was my tendency to interrupt others. In the heat of discussions, my excitement and passion would often lead me to cut off my colleague's mid-sentence. Recognizing this as a counterproductive habit, I implemented a simple yet effective strategy. Whenever I felt the urge to interrupt, I would gently press my lips together, taking a moment to fully process what was being said before formulating my response.

This technique not only curbed my interrupting behaviour but also gave me the opportunity to truly listen and engage with my colleagues' ideas. As a result, I was able to offer more thoughtful and constructive feedback, fostering a more collaborative and respectful work environment.

PS Thanks VB for the tip

Another area of growth for me was in the realm of difficult conversations. Initially, I avoided these uncomfortable situations, fearing that they would damage the positive relationships I had built with my colleagues. However, I soon realized that by shying away from these conversations, I was potentially hindering the professional development of my peers and stunting my own growth as well.

With a newfound commitment to open and honest communication, I began to approach these difficult discussions with empathy and a focus on constructive feedback. I found that by providing my colleagues with candid yet compassionate guidance, I was able to help them identify areas for improvement and unlock their full potential. This, in turn, strengthened the overall effectiveness of our team and bolstered my own confidence as a communicator.

The journey of refining my communication skills has been transformative, not only in my professional life but also in my personal relationships. By practicing active listening, thoughtful expression, and the courage to have difficult conversations, I have become a more confident, impactful, and influential communicator. This evolution has positively impacted my ability to collaborate, navigate complex interpersonal dynamics, and contribute meaningfully to the success of my organization

In fact, the benefits of my improved communication skills have even extended to my personal life. For instance, I now have the confidence to approach my next-door neighbour and politely request that they refrain from playing their electric guitar too loudly after 10 o'clock. Previously, I may have avoided this uncomfortable conversation, but now I understand the importance of addressing such issues directly and constructively.

the concept of continuous learning and skill development

Let's explore this next part of the book, highlighting the importance of never stopping the pursuit of knowledge and self-improvement, as well as the value of skill sharing within the workplace.

Embracing a Mindset of Continuous Learning

As young professionals, it's easy to fall into the trap of complacency, resting on the laurels of our existing skills and knowledge. However, the most successful individuals understand that the journey of learning and self-development is never truly complete. By maintaining a mindset of continuous learning, we open ourselves up to new perspectives, innovative approaches, and opportunities for growth.

In my own experience, I've found that even the most familiar tasks or processes can often be improved upon. Whether it's a more efficient way of organizing my work, a novel problem-solving technique, or a cutting-edge software tool, there is always something new to discover. Embracing this mindset of continuous learning has allowed me to stay ahead of the curve, adapt to changing demands, and consistently deliver high-quality work.

The Power of Skill Sharing

One of the most valuable aspects of this continuous learning journey has been the concept of "skill sharing" within my workplace. Rather than hoarding knowledge or skills, my colleagues and I have made a conscious effort to openly share our expertise and insights with one another.

This collaborative approach has fostered a culture of mutual growth and development. When I learn a new technique or discover a better way of doing something, I make it a point to share this information with my team. Likewise, my colleagues are eager to do the same, creating a dynamic exchange of knowledge and skills.

The benefits of this skill-sharing environment are numerous. Not only does it enhance the overall competence and capabilities of our team, but it also promotes a sense of camaraderie and shared purpose. By learning from one another, we're able to tackle challenges more effectively, identify innovative solutions, and ultimately deliver greater value to our organization.

Moreover, the act of teaching and sharing one's skills has a remarkable way of reinforcing and solidifying our own learning. As the saying goes, "the best way to learn is to teach." By taking the time to explain a concept or demonstrate a technique to our colleagues, we deepen our own understanding and recognition of the underlying principles.

Continuous Skill Development through Formal and Informal Means

In addition to the organic skill sharing that takes place within our team, I've also made a concerted effort to seek out formal and informal avenues for continuous skill development. This might include enrolling in online development or sitting down and searching on the internet best practices.

The beauty of this multifaceted approach is that it allows me to tailor my learning to my specific needs and interests. Whether I'm looking to enhance my data analysis capabilities, improve my public speaking skills, or gain a deeper understanding of emerging industry trends, there is always a relevant learning opportunity available.

By embracing this mindset of continuous learning and skill development, I've not only expanded my professional toolkit but also cultivated a greater sense of adaptability and resilience. In an ever-evolving business landscape, the ability to continuously learn, grow, and share knowledge has become an invaluable asset.

As I look ahead, I'm excited to see where this journey of lifelong learning will take me. The potential for growth and self-improvement is truly limitless, and I'm committed to leveraging every opportunity to enhance my skills

Networking and building relationships

The importance of networking, building relationships, and fostering a collaborative work environment is a crucial aspect of professional development. Let's dive into this next part of the book and explore why team camaraderie, involvement, and mutual learning are so valuable.

The Power of Networking and Relationship Building

As young professionals, it's easy to become laser-focused on our individual tasks and responsibilities, but the reality is that the most successful individuals understand the immense value of networking and building meaningful relationships within the workplace.

When we take the time to connect with our colleagues, share our experiences, and learn from one another, we unlock a world of opportunities. Not only do these relationships provide a valuable support system, but they also serve as conduits for knowledge sharing, skill development, and even potential career advancement.

Encouraging Team Involvement and Collaboration

One of the hallmarks of a thriving work culture is a sense of team camaraderie and shared ownership. By actively encouraging our colleagues to get involved in new projects, volunteer for additional responsibilities, or simply engage in open dialogue, we foster a collaborative environment that benefits everyone.

This spirit of involvement and cooperation serves several important purposes. First, it allows individuals to expand their skill sets and gain exposure to new areas of the business, ultimately enhancing their overall value to the organization. Additionally, it cultivates a sense of shared purpose and investment, where everyone feels empowered to contribute to the team's success.

Moreover, when we actively invite our colleagues to participate and share their unique perspectives, we demonstrate a genuine interest in their professional growth and development. This, in turn, strengthens the bonds of trust and respect within the team, leading to more effective communication, problem-solving, and ultimately, superior outcomes.

Learning from Peers and Mentors

One of the most rewarding aspects of building strong relationships in the workplace is the opportunity to learn from our peers and mentors. By tapping into the knowledge and expertise of those around us, we can accelerate our own skill development and gain valuable insights that might otherwise elude us.

Whether it's seeking guidance from a seasoned colleague on a specific project, or engaging in a mentorship program to explore new career paths, these relationships serve as conduits for continuous learning and growth. By being open to learning from others, we not only improve our own capabilities but also contribute to the overall knowledge-sharing culture within the organization.

Equally important, the act of sharing our own skills and experiences with our peers can be just as valuable. When we take the time to mentor or coach others, we solidify our own understanding of the subject matter while also paying forward the support and guidance that we've received throughout our careers.

Cultivating a Collaborative and Connected Workplace

By embracing the power of networking, team involvement, and mutual learning, we can collectively create a workplace that is vibrant, supportive, and conducive to professional development. When people feel connected, valued, and empowered to contribute, the entire organization benefits from increased productivity, innovation, and a shared sense of purpose.

As young professionals, it's our responsibility to be proactive in building these relationships and fostering a collaborative work environment. Whether it's volunteering for a new project, offering to mentor a junior colleague, or simply making an effort to connect with our peers, every small step we take can have a significant impact on the overall culture and success of our organization.

Remember, the journey of professional growth is not one that we must navigate alone.

Embracing Adaptability and Agility in the Retail Landscape

(Being ok with new!)

The retail industry is a dynamic and ever-changing landscape, where the ability to adapt and respond to new trends, technologies, and customer demands is paramount to success. As young professionals navigating this fast-paced environment, the development of adaptability and agility has become essential for both our personal growth and the success of our organizations.

Adapting to Transformative Trends in Fashion and Shopping Experiences

In the fashion retail sector, we have witnessed a profound transformation in recent years. From the emergence of new fashion trends to the introduction of innovative shopping experiences, the industry has had to constantly evolve to meet the changing needs and expectations of our customers.

One such example is the rise of click-and-collect services, where customers can order products online and pick them up in-store. This shift has required us to rethink our store operations, inventory management, and customer service strategies. Similarly, the introduction of self-service kiosks and automated checkout systems has challenged our traditional understanding of the in-store shopping experience.

Embracing these changes and learning to adapt quickly has been crucial for our continued success. By approaching these new initiatives with an open mindset and a willingness to learn, we have been able to not only implement them effectively but also encourage and develop our teams to embrace these transformative elements of the business.

Fostering a Culture of Adaptability and Agility

Adaptability and agility are not just individual traits, but also essential components of a thriving organizational culture. As leaders and mentors, it is our responsibility to cultivate an environment that empowers our teams to be responsive to change and proactive in their approach to problem-solving.

This begins with leading by example, demonstrating our own ability to adapt to new challenges and embrace innovative solutions. By sharing our experiences, both successes, and failures, we can inspire our colleagues to adopt a similar mindset, one that is open to learning, experimenting, and continuously improving.

Furthermore, we must create opportunities for our teams to engage with and contribute to the evolution of our business. By soliciting their feedback, encouraging their participation in new initiatives, and providing the necessary support and resources, we can harness the collective intelligence and creativity of our workforce to drive meaningful change.

Adapting to Changing Customer Demands and Preferences

Perhaps one of the most significant drivers of adaptability in the retail industry is the constant evolution of customer preferences and shopping behaviours. As professionals, we must remain vigilant in monitoring these shifts and be prepared to pivot our strategies accordingly.

Whether it's adapting our product assortments to cater to emerging fashion trends, optimizing our digital platforms to enhance the online shopping experience, or revamping our in-store layouts to better serve our customers' needs, our ability to adapt and respond quickly can mean the difference between success and stagnation.

By fostering a culture of adaptability and agility, we empower our teams to be proactive, innovative, and customer-centric in their approach. This, in turn, allows us to stay ahead of the curve, anticipate and meet the evolving demands of our target market, and position our organizations for long-term growth and success.

Embracing the Challenges and Opportunities of Change

The retail industry's constant state of flux can be both exhilarating and daunting. However, by cultivating a mindset of adaptability and agility, we can transform these challenges into opportunities for personal and professional development.

As we navigate the ever-changing landscape of fashion and shopping experiences, let us approach each new initiative, technology, or customer preference with a sense of curiosity, openness, and a willingness to learn. By doing so, we not only ensure the continued success of our organizations but also unlock our own potential for growth and innovation.

The power of Emotional Intelligence and Self-Awareness

As young professionals, it's easy to become laser-focused on the technical aspects of our roles, prioritizing hard skills and quantifiable achievements. However, the reality is that our ability to succeed in the workplace is heavily influenced by our emotional intelligence (EQ) – our capacity to recognize, understand, and manage our own emotions, as well as empathize with the emotions of others.

Developing Self-Awareness

At the core of emotional intelligence is self-awareness – the deep understanding of our own emotions, strengths, weaknesses, and emotional triggers. By taking the time to reflect on our internal experiences, we can gain valuable insights that allow us to better manage our responses and interactions with colleagues, clients, and superiors.

When we are self-aware, we are better equipped to identify our emotional reactions in real-time and make conscious choices about how to channel those emotions in a productive manner. This not only helps us avoid potentially damaging outbursts or knee-jerk reactions but also enables us to approach challenging situations with a more measured and empathetic mindset.

Practicing Empathy and Emotional Regulation

Alongside self-awareness, the development of empathy and emotional regulation are crucial components of emotional intelligence. By cultivating the ability to understand and share the feelings of others, we can build stronger, more meaningful connections with our colleagues. This, in turn, fosters a work environment characterized by trust, collaboration, and mutual support.

Moreover, the skill of emotional regulation – the capacity to manage our own emotions and impulses – allows us to navigate personal dynamics more effectively. When faced with stressful or contentious situations, emotionally intelligent individuals are better equipped to remain calm, communicate clearly, and find constructive solutions that address the underlying needs and concerns of all parties involved.

Acknowledging Our Humanity

As young professionals, it's important to remember that we are not merely robots or automatons tasked with the execution of our duties. We are human beings, with complex emotions, experiences, and personal lives that inevitably influence our professional performance and well-being.

By acknowledging and embracing our humanity, we create space for empathy, understanding, and compassion – both for ourselves and for our colleagues. It's okay to have a bad day, to feel overwhelmed, or to struggle with certain challenges. The key is to develop the self-awareness and emotional regulation skills to navigate these experiences in a constructive manner.

Cultivating Emotional Intelligence for Professional and Personal Growth

The development of emotional intelligence is not a one-time event but rather a continuous journey of self-discovery and growth. By prioritizing the cultivation of self-awareness, empathy, and emotional regulation, we unlock a powerful set of skills that can elevate our performance, strengthen our relationships, and contribute to the overall success and well-being of our organizations.

As young professionals, let us embrace this journey with enthusiasm and a willingness to learn. By recognizing the importance of emotional intelligence and incorporating it into our daily lives, we can position ourselves for long-term success, both in our careers and in our personal lives.

concise tips for developing self-awareness and emotional intelligence

1. **Practice self-reflection:**

   - Set aside regular time for introspection.

   - Examine your thoughts, feelings, and behaviours.

   - Identify patterns, triggers, and areas for growth.

2. **Seek feedback:**

   - Ask colleagues, managers, and mentors for honest feedback.

   - Listen without defensiveness and look for areas for improvement.

   - Express gratitude for the insights provided.

3. **Cultivate mindfulness:**

- Be present and attuned to your emotions in the moment.

   - Observe your reactions without judgment.

   - Pause before responding to challenging situations.

4. **Develop empathy**:

   - Actively listen to understand others' perspectives.

   - Imagine yourself in their shoes and consider their feelings.

   - Respond with compassion and a desire to help.

5. **Practice emotional regulation**:

   - Identify and name your emotions as they arise.

   - Develop strategies to manage strong emotions, such as deep breathing.

   - Communicate your feelings in a constructive manner.

6. **Embrace continuous learning**:

- Read books and articles on self-awareness and interpersonal skills.

- Apply new insights and techniques to your daily life.

Remember, developing self-awareness and emotional intelligence is an ongoing process. Consistency, patience, and a growth mindset are key to unlocking your full potential.

Prioritizing Work-Life Balance

As young professionals, it's easy to become consumed by the demands of our careers, often at the expense of our personal well-being. However, the most successful individuals understand that striking a healthy balance between work and life is essential for long-term success and fulfilment.

Establishing Healthy Habits and Routines

The foundation of work-life balance lies in the cultivation of healthy habits and routines. This might include regular exercise, a balanced diet, consistent sleep patterns, and intentional time for relaxation and leisure activities.

(I know for meany of us a healthy start to the day is coffee and more coffee!!!)

By prioritizing our physical and mental well-being, we not only enhance our overall productivity and performance but also build the resilience necessary to navigate the inevitable challenges and stressors of our professional lives.

Managing Stress and Maintaining a Positive Mindset

Stress is an unavoidable aspect of the workplace, but it is how we choose to manage it that makes all the difference. Developing effective stress management techniques, such as mindfulness practices, time management strategies, and boundary-setting, can help us maintain a positive and realistic mindset.

It's important to remember that a positive mindset does not mean ignoring or suppressing negative emotions. Rather, it's about cultivating a balanced perspective that acknowledges both the challenges and the opportunities inherent in our work and personal lives.

Prioritizing Work-Life Balance to Avoid Burnout

One of the most significant threats to our well-being is the risk of burnout – a state of physical, emotional, and mental exhaustion that can have devastating consequences on our personal and professional lives.

By prioritizing work-life balance and setting clear boundaries, we can proactively mitigate the risk of burnout and ensure that we remain engaged, motivated, and capable of delivering our best work. This might involve setting limits on work hours, taking regular breaks, and learning to delegate or say "no" when necessary.

Fostering a Culture of Well-Being

As young professionals, we have the power to influence the work culture within our organizations. By leading by example and advocating for policies and practices that support employee well-being, we can create an environment that empowers everyone to thrive.

This might include initiatives such as wellness programs, flexible work arrangements, and open dialogues about the importance of self-care. By fostering a culture that values work-life balance and overall well-being, we not only contribute to the success of our organizations but also inspire others to prioritize their own health and happiness.

Embracing the Journey of Work-Life Balance

Achieving true work-life balance is not a one-time destination but rather an ongoing journey of self-discovery and adjustment. As our lives and priorities evolve, we must be willing to continuously re-evaluate our habits, routines, and boundaries to ensure that we are maintaining a healthy and sustainable balance.

By embracing this journey with a growth mindset, we can unlock the full potential of our personal and professional lives, ultimately leading to greater fulfilment, productivity, and success.

A Personal Story of Finding Balance

When I first started my career, I was eager to prove myself and be a dedicated, hardworking professional. In my eagerness to excel, I found myself overworking and neglecting other important aspects of my life. I would bring work home, check emails late into the night, and sacrifice time with my family in the pursuit of professional success.

At first, this relentless drive felt productive and fulfilling. I was making great strides in my career, and it was gratifying to see the results of my efforts. However, over time, the constant grind began to take a toll. I started feeling exhausted, both physically and mentally. My relationships suffered as I became increasingly detached and unavailable to my loved ones.

It was a wake-up call when I realized I was on the verge of burnout. I recognized that I needed to take a step back and re-evaluate my priorities. Establishing clear boundaries between my work and personal life became crucial. I made a conscious effort to stop working once I had clocked out for the day, and I made it a point to be fully present with my family during that time.

This shift wasn't easy at first. I had to fight the urge to constantly check my phone or tackle just one more task. But as I persisted, I began to see the immense benefits of this work-life balance. My productivity at work actually improved, as I was able to focus more intently during my designated work hours. More importantly, my relationships and overall well-being flourished as I made time for the people and activities that truly mattered to me.

The journey to finding balance is an ongoing one, and there are still times when I have to consciously remind myself to step away from work. But I've learned that it's not only okay, but essential, to set boundaries and prioritize my mental and physical health. By doing so, I've not only become a more well-rounded and fulfilled individual, but I've also become a more effective and valuable professional.

Tom's end notes

As I revisited the concept of accountability, I found myself inspired to write this book—a journey that has been both enlightening and transformative. Throughout this process, I realized that my passion for sharing experiences that can positively impact others is deeply rooted in the incredible guidance I received from my boss. Her introduction to accountability and consistency changed my perspective and, ultimately, my life.

In writing this book, I aimed to pass on that same gift of insight and empowerment. It is my hope that the lessons I've learned and shared resonate with you, just as they did with me. Accountability is not merely a buzzword; it is a powerful tool that can lead to personal growth, stronger relationships, and a fulfilling professional life.

Thank you for joining me on this journey. May the insights you gain from this book inspire you to embrace accountability and consistency in your own life, unlocking your potential and fostering a culture of growth and support. I encourage you to take these concepts to heart and implement them in your daily practices. The path to accountability is a continuous journey, and I hope it brings you as much clarity and fulfilment as it has brought me.

Here's to your journey of accountability and the positive changes it will create!

One Last Word of Gratitude

As I reflect on my journey and all that I have learnt, I would be remiss if I didn't take a moment to express my deep gratitude to my work family. To my leaders and my colleagues, you know who you are - I wouldn't be where I am now without your unwavering support and understanding.

Your compassion and commitment to fostering a truly amazing culture, By leading by example and championing the importance of self-care, you have not only enriched my own life but have also set the tone for our entire place of work. I am honoured to be a part of a team that values each and every one of us individually.

To my incredible leader, in particular, your unwavering support and mentorship have been instrumental in my personal and professional growth. Your trust in my abilities, even when I doubted myself, has been a constant source of motivation and empowerment.

I am deeply grateful for the role you all have played in my journey. Your understanding, flexibility, and genuine concern for my well-being have not only allowed me to thrive in my career but have also enriched my life beyond the confines of the office. I am truly fortunate to have such a remarkable work family by my side.

Thank you, from the bottom of my heart, for your invaluable support Your kindness and compassion have left an indelible mark, and I will carry these lessons with me as I continue to navigate the ever-evolving landscape of work and life.

notes

www.ingramcontent.com/pod-product-compliance
Lightning Source LLC
Chambersburg PA
CBHW071946210526
45479CB00002B/827